Haik and Home Truths

*Haikus and home truths:
some may leave you pondering,
some may make you smile.*

By Paul Middleton

Haikus

Copyright © (Paul Middleton 2019)

All rights reserved

No part of this book may be reproduced in any form by photocopying or any electronic or mechanical means, including information storage or retrieval systems, without permission in writing from both the copyright owner and the publisher of the book.

All characters are fictional. Any similarity to any action person is purely coincidental.

ISBN: 9781784566869

Paperback

First published 2019 by UPFRONT PUBLISHING
Peterborough, England.

An environmentally friendly book printed and bound in England by www.printondemand-worldwide.com

*In so many ways,
knowing and unwittingly,
you have rescued me.*

CONTENTS

Haiku	v
Introduction	vi
Section 1: Japan	1
Section 2: Nearer Home	22
Section 3: Reflections	45
Section 4: Which Way?	64

Haiku

Haiku a Japanese poem in three lines of 5, 7, 5 syllables

In 17th century Japan, Matsuo Basho was one of two masters who transformed the art of Japanese poetry by giving new emphasis to the first introductory scene-setting verse of a traditional poem form, the *renku*. Whereas previously this opening verse, termed *hokku*, had always been understood in the context of the whole composition, Basho and his followers elevated it by giving it stand alone importance.

Basho used this style extensively in his own prose writing, often with humour, placing *hokku* almost as punctuation marks in his travelogues, the best known of which was called "Narrow Roads to the Interior." *

Basho continued to be an inspiration in Japanese poetry into the 19th century at which time his emphasis on playful wit and thoughtful reflection was developed further and the term *Haiku* came into general use.

Basho was deified by the imperial Japanese government and has continued to be revered in Japan, as well as becoming perhaps the one name from classical Japanese literature familiar throughout the world.

- Matsuo Basho *Narrow Roads to the Interior and other writings* (translated by Sam Hamill) Shambhala Pocket Library 2019

Introduction

The idea for this collection originated during a trip to Japan in April 2019. This was in every way a revelation, a wonderful and transforming experience. Unable to sleep well for much of the trip, however, I spent the wakeful hours seeing if I could submit myself to the discipline of the haiku poem structure. Having previously been somewhat resistant to the idea of writing to a formula, I was surprised by how much I enjoyed the challenge and began to try composing a haiku for each stage of our adventure.

I also enjoyed the freedom that Basho's example gave of writing these short pithy thoughts about trivial as well as more serious topics, their brevity making them all the more memorable.

So, when I returned to England, I continued to use the haiku formula, applying it to various aspects of life at home, shifting between physical and inner, reflective journeying. In truth it became something of an obsession, seeking out five and seven syllable phrases wherever I went, whatever I happened to be reading!

I hope those who pick up this volume will enjoy the rhythm of the haiku structure as much as I have and even be inspired to try some themselves, perhaps revisiting past schoolroom experiences with a fresh eye.

"Listen to your life…..
All moments are key moments…..
Life itself is grace."

(Frederick Buechner *Now and Then* Harper One 1983, 87)

August 2019

Japan

*Sumo, samurai,
guided gardens, tower views:
ancient past meets new.*

*Leaving Tokyo,
Fuji hiding, teasing – there!
A snow-capped icon.*

Crow Castle brooding –
five floors, steep stairs ascending,
boasts blossom delight.

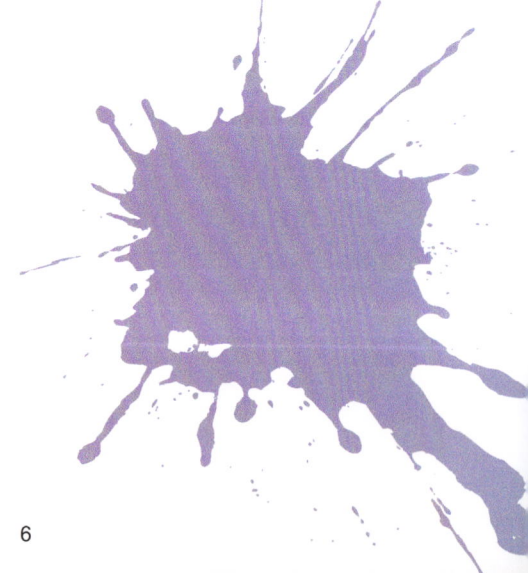

Snow slip-sliding slog,
pine clad hills, black bear aware,
cobbled paths speak age.

*Narai ghost town feel
hides warmth and welcome within.
Artist's talents shared.*

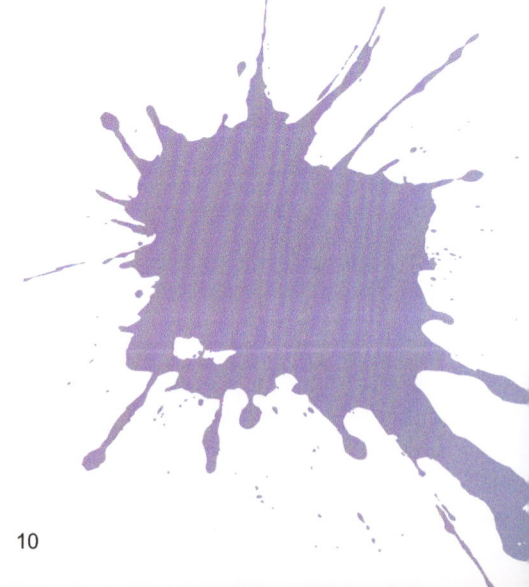

*Futon rested and
fine dining, Japanese style.
Hot spring baths refresh.*

We gather, we gaze,
delicate beauty displayed –
soft benediction.

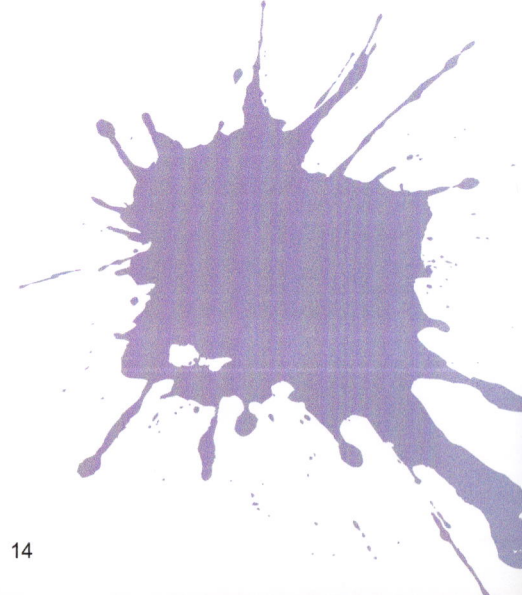

*Three geikos dancing,
skilled in arts to entertain.
Discreet party hosts.*

Ordered actions calm.
Together in harmony.
One life, one meeting.

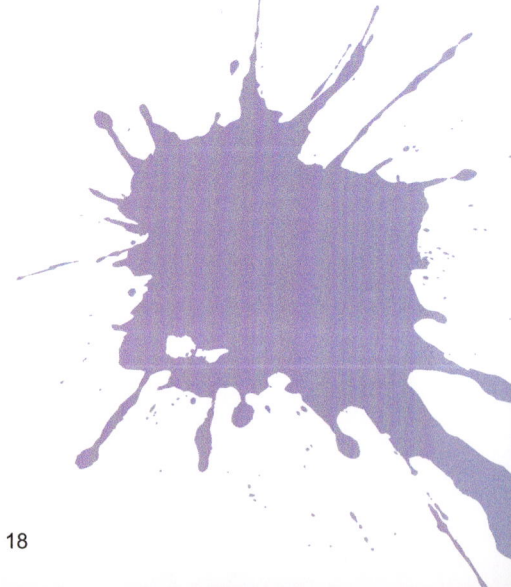

*Such warmth and welcome,
shared knowledge and love of place,
insight with humour.*

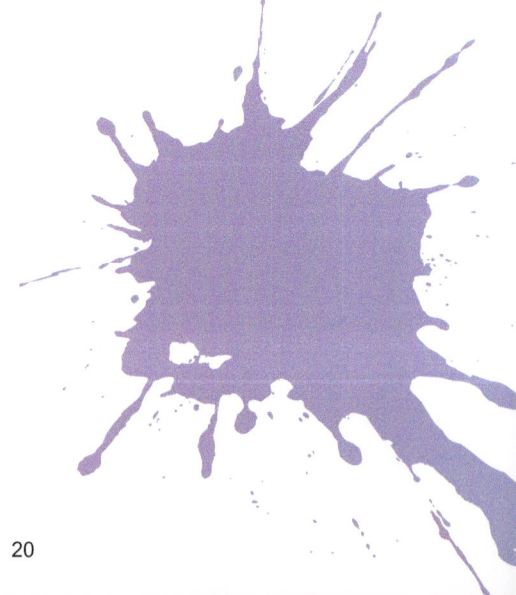

Nearer Home

*Fluttering fledgling,
fatter than your parent bird,
"Find your own fat worm!"*

*In greenhouse nurtured,
plants speak of new life surging,
gardens to adorn.*

Strawberry Wars

Fine handsome blackbird,
acquainted, compost digging,
thought you were my friend.

Strawberries ripe'ning,
tasty fruit to come, but then –
blackbird got there first.

Strawberries guarded,
netted, garden dawn patrol –
pest bird strikes again!

Crisis looming fast,
fresh approach now much needed –
what else can I do?

A new perspective:
Much pleasure birds bring, and so,
share garden's bounty.

*Great pleasure I find
autumn-time blackberrying.
Would you like to come?*

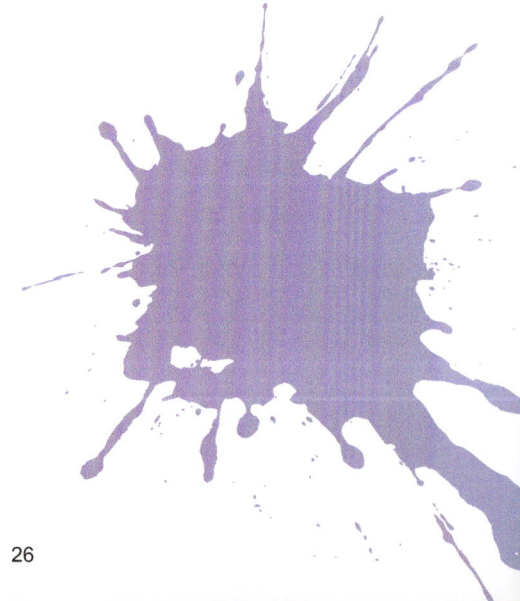

*Digging down the fen,
bank, musket range exploring,
friends and summer wine.*

*Testament to God,
masons built to monks' design,
grandeur, strong to last.*

Photo: Peterborough Cathedral with permission

Eyeless watch-tower,
recalls Oswald's relic arm,
guarding tranquil space.

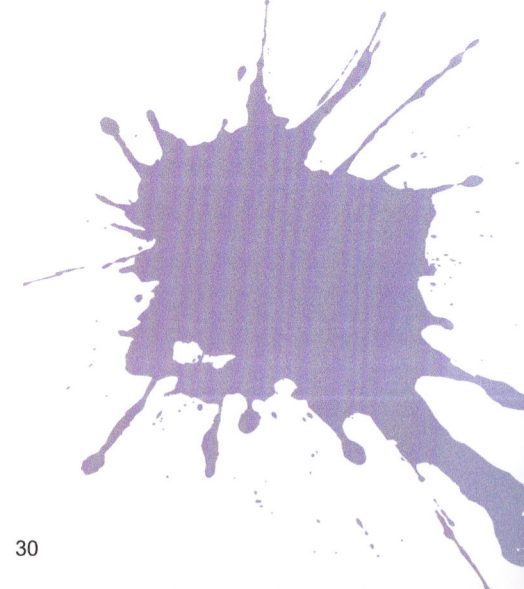

*Commonwealth statement,
rising at cathedral's fall,
now gives hospice care.*

Stamford streets delight: Georgian elegance framing a cultural hub.

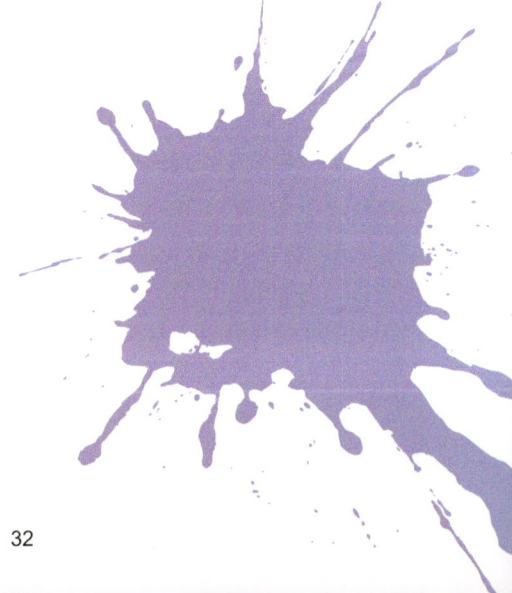

Photo: John Mitchell

*All Saints spire soars high,
drawing pilgrims, peace within,
thankful for God's touch.*

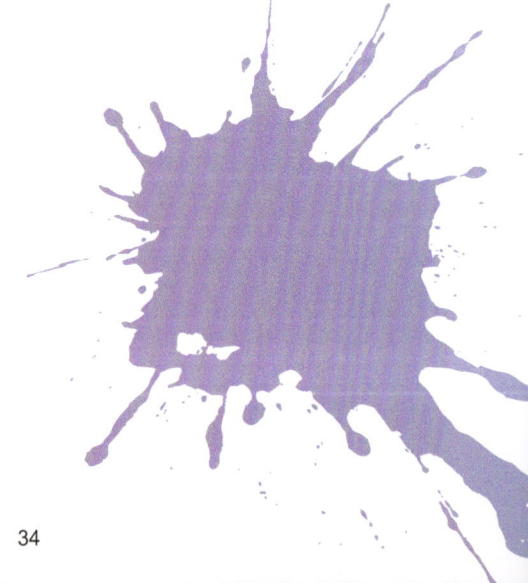

Photo: John Mitchell

*Burghley Park's surprise -
water fountains, sculpture, space,
tea, coffee and cake.*

Photo: John Mitchell

*Lathkill, Matlock Bath,
Bakewell tart, homity pie -
Derby Dales' delights.*

*In Bakewell All Saints,
a unique and special place,
this pilgrim's refuge.*

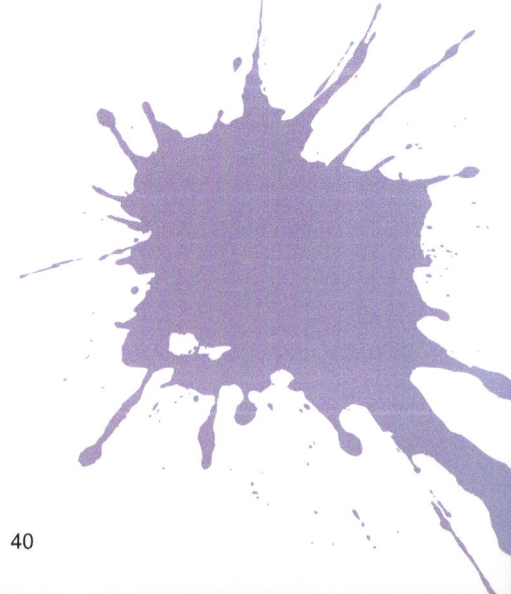

*Melton market stroll,
pleasure giving through the years,
pork pie rewarding.*

*Wandlebury walks,
sport of kings a memory
masking deeper past.*

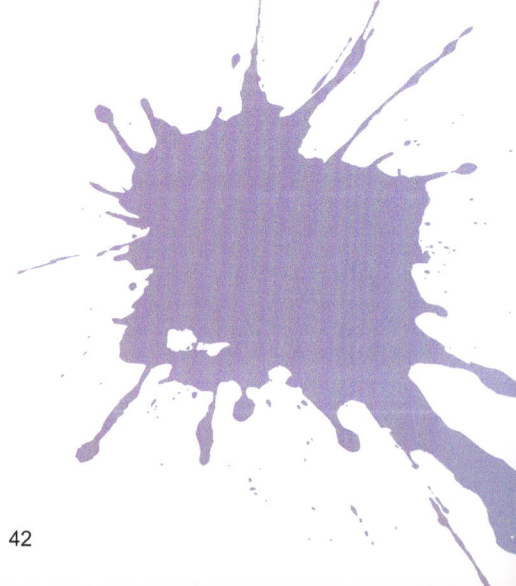

*At Whitby, waking,
gulls gather with raucous calls,
cacophonous din.*

*Buzzing of the bees,
breeze wafting sun-soaked arbour,
thatch cottage retreat.*

Reflections

*Here I am standing
at the edge of becoming,
drawn forwards and back.*

*Just before you speak
consider, is it helpful?
Is it kind and true?*

After Canon John King

In times of trial, certainties gone. Not lost, just waiting to be found.

*After so much hurt,
trust may be the hardest thing.
Say yes to new life.*

*Dark can be scary,
misgivings and threats crowd in
– look up at the stars!*

*With night vision on,
find true treasures in darkness,
open to the night.*

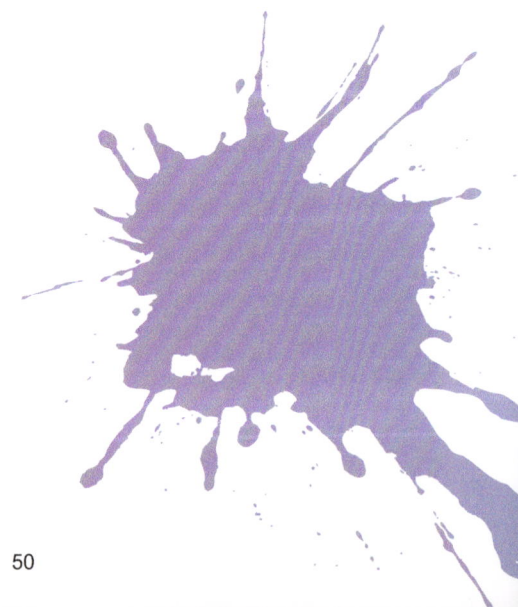

*Treasures in darkness –
a mystery so profound.
Hope keeps us searching.*

*Treasures in darkness,
havens of light in distress –
and you have been one.*

*Into the garden,
those pests amongst the flowers -
just like life itself.*

*Fenland hermitage
focus for peace and healing,
found in shared silence.*

*So many questions,
bring us up sharp: "What is it
that you think you have?"*

The roots I draw on, nourished past, now companion to new beginnings.

*"Silence is golden"?
Sometimes! and most certainly
pregnant with rich gifts.*

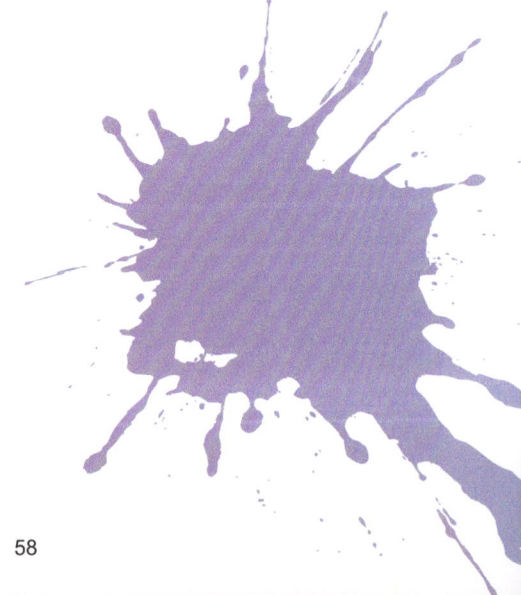

*Standing at the edge,
logic says, "Retreat! Stand back!
How then will you fly?*

*Life is full of pain,
but here is the mystery,
also full of love.*

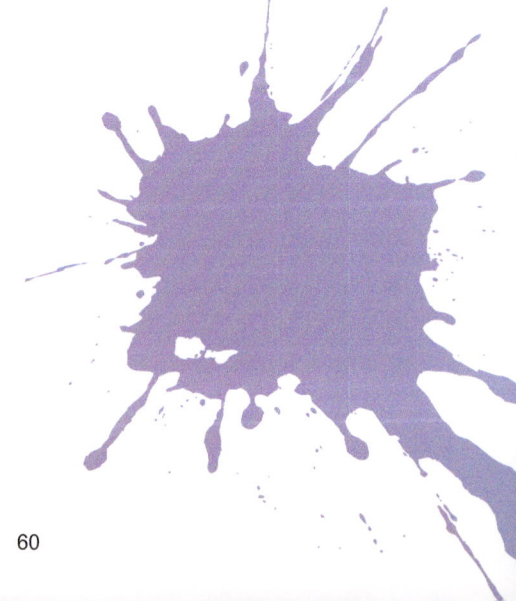

*At once natural,
transforming, warming and true,
our very first kiss.*

*Hidden by seasons,
my love will last forever,
bursting forth again.*

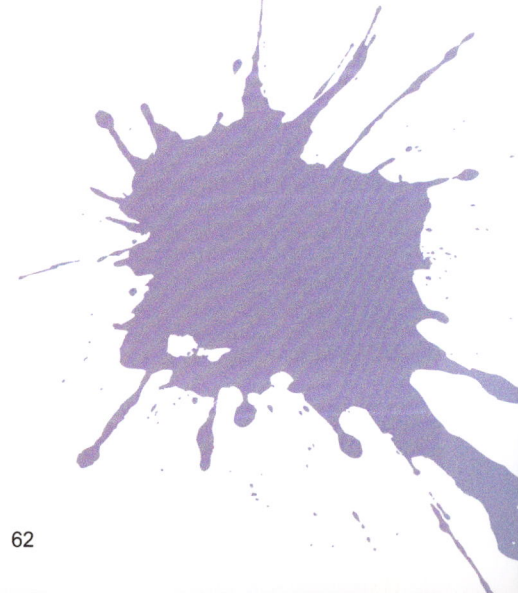

Which Way?

Election day

Who should we vote for?
Intelligent, witty, bright –
but have they wisdom?

So how can we know?
Confused, how do we discern?
To whom shall we turn?

Honest endeavour,
integrity, showing love
in selfless action.

These are the hallmarks
of a servant who has earned
respect and support.

*Is this what I seek
at the end of my searching,
lost soul that I am?*

*Freed from all worry,
my trust and hope in my Lord,
friend, guide and master.*

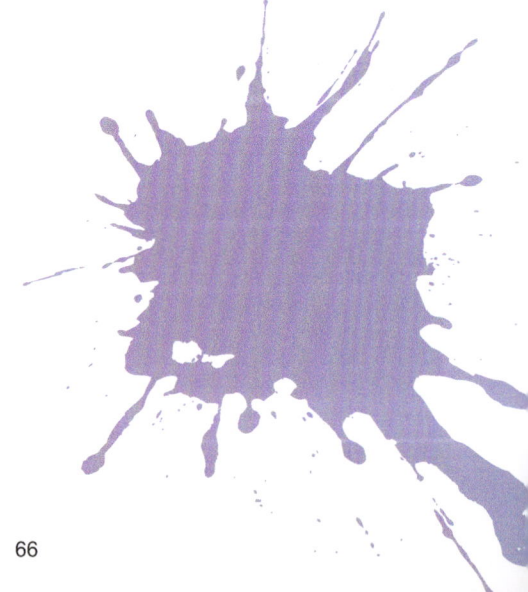

*Celtic Daily Prayer –
a discipline, solace, guide,
healing to the soul.*

*Hard choice at lunchtime,
each with distinctive appeal:
cherry or cheese scone?*

*Sleeping or waking,
God holds you in His embrace.
In Him we can trust.*

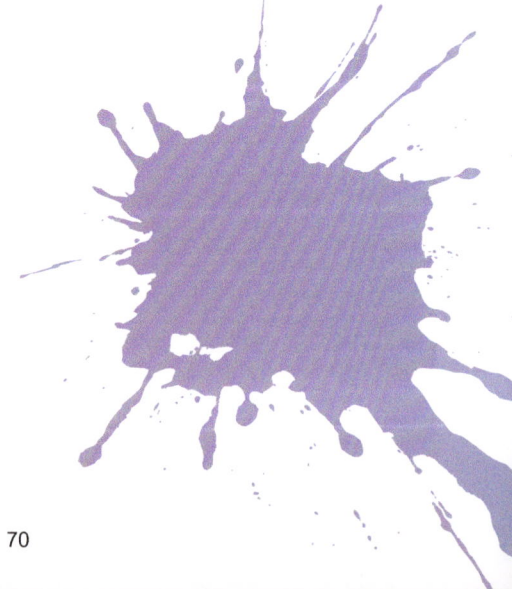

Heaven and Earth

Ludmila meet my
Linda who's been here a while,
and there's much to do.

****

When the best are gone,
what do we, who now are left,
do before we die?

What is there to say?
It is as bad as it feels
and the pain cuts deep.

There is no purpose.
A beautiful life cut short;
family wreckage.

The hurt in this world –
how can we bear all this pain?
I will hope in God.

*Each day is a gift,
so let us inhabit it,
fully present, now.*

*Action and silence
Make life's daily ebb and flow,
rhythm of the tides.*

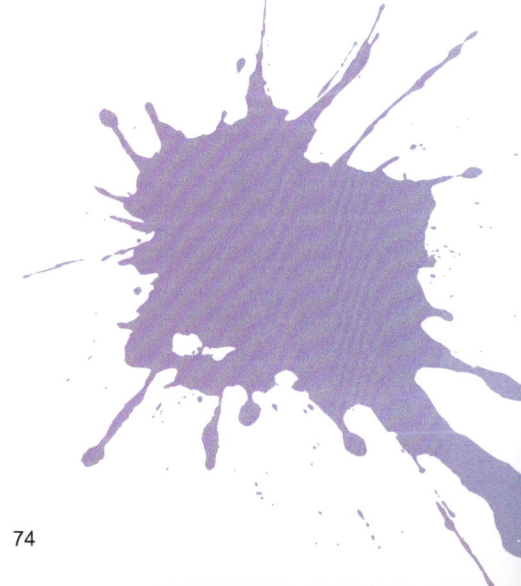